CRITICAL ACCLAIM

"Premature ejaculation is one of the most common sexual dysfunctions in men and is the easiest to treat. Such men often develop secondary impotence and reduced sexual desire, and their partners often develop secondary anorgasmia or reduced desire, leading in turn to marked marital dissatisfaction and even divorce. This simply, clearly written book should be most helpful to sufferers from this disorder, either as a self-help program, or in conjunction with treatment by a reputable sex therapist."   —WILLIAM S. SIMPSON, M.D.
Director, Center for Sexual Health
The Menninger Clinic

"Dr. Kaplan has presented a lucid, direct and straightforward approach to a very troubling problem. Her book is designed to help those with premature ejaculation by enabling them to help themselves. The book is very readable and the directions are presented clearly and understandably."
—CAROL C. NADELSON, M.D.
Professor and Vice Chairman, Department of Psychiatry
Tufts University

"This is a very practical, down-to-earth book, and it provides realistic hope, is supportive, and has good illustrative vignettes. One of the most helpful parts of the book is that it affirms the commonality and normalcy of the challenge of premature ejaculation as opposed to a 'sickness' view. . . . I do like the idea of the chapter entitled 'How To Be Your Own Sex Therapist.' As a person who has been a sex therapist for more than 18 years, I celebrate this idea in terms of specific suggestions and the empowerment someone can have by understanding commonality as well as specific suggestions in terms of 'self-treatment.'"   —RALPH H. EARLE, Ph.D.
Psychological Counseling Services, Ltd.
Scottsdale, Arizona

"Only an experienced professional can give open and frank information, which is paramount in overcoming problems. This book is important as it gives the single as well as the coupled man the possibility of learning the simple exercises which are the critical elements in overcoming PE. It is a non-frightening, thoughtful book which, with its many suggestions and pieces of advice, will make any man—even the one without 'problems'—a more considerate lover."
—GORM WAGNER, M.D., Ph.D.
University of Copenhagen

BOOKS BY HELEN SINGER KAPLAN, M.D., Ph.D.

Published by Brunner/Mazel

The New Sex Therapy: Active Treatment of
    Sexual Dysfunctions (1974, 1981)

Disorders of Sexual Desire (1979)

The Evaluation of Sexual Disorders: Psychological
    and Medical Aspects (with M. Horwith, M.D.,
    J. Imperato-McGinley, M.D., S. A. Kaufman, M.D.,
    E. Leiter, M.D., A. Melman, M.D., &
    J. M. Reckler, M.D.) (1983)

Sexual Aversion, Sexual Phobias, and Panic Disorder
(with a chapter by Donald F. Klein, M.D.) (1987)

The Illustrated Manual of Sex Therapy (1975).
    Second Edition (1987)

Published by Simon & Schuster

Making Sense of Sex: The New Facts about Sex
    and Love for Young People (1979)

The Real Truth about Women and AIDS: How to
    Eliminate the Risks without Giving up Love
    and Sex (1987)

HOW TO OVERCOME PREMATURE EJACULATION

By

Helen Singer Kaplan, M.D., Ph.D.

Director of the Human Sexuality Program
The New York Hospital–Cornell Medical Center

Routledge
Taylor & Francis Group
New York   London

Published in 1989 by
Routledge
Taylor & Francis Group
270 Madison Avenue
New York, NY 10016

Published in Great Britain by
Routledge
Taylor & Francis Group
2 Park Square
Milton Park, Abingdon
Oxon OX14 4RN

Printed in the United States of America on acid-free paper

International Standard Book Number-10: 0-87630-542-7 (Softcover)
International Standard Book Number-13: 978-0-87630-542-3 (Softcover)
Library of Congress Card Number 88-35193

Figure 2, p. 25, by Barbara Rankin, originally appeared in **The New Sex Therapy: Active Treatment of Sexual Dysfunctions**, © 1974 by Helen Singer Kaplan, M.D., Ph.D.

Figures 3, 4, and 5, pp. 51, 55, and 58, by David Passalacqua, originally appeared in **The Illustrated Manual of Sex Therapy**, © 1975 by Helen Singer Kaplan, M.D., Ph.D.
Cover design by Wendy Kassner

Library of Congress Cataloging-in-Publication Data

Kaplan, Helen Singer.
   How to overcome premature ejaculation.
   Bibliography: p. 117.
   ISBN 0-87630-542-7
   1. Premature ejaculation—Treatment.   2. Sex therapy.   I. Title.
RC560.P73K36   1989
616.6'93   88-35193

Visit the Taylor & Francis Web site at
http://www.taylorandfrancis.com

and the Routledge Web site at
http://www.routledge.com

Contents

Illustrations

HOW TO OVERCOME PREMATURE EJACULATION

CHAPTER 1

Premature Ejaculation (PE) Can Be Cured

Before the advent of modern sex therapy, the great majority of men who suffered from premature ejaculation were stuck with their problem for life. In those days, the chances of finding a cure were exceedingly slim because the cause of premature ejaculation was not understood and no one knew how to treat this disorder correctly. Until recently, doctors were still recommending anesthetic ointments, which don't work, or psychoanalysis, which, although requiring a great deal of time and money (usually three to five office visits a week for a matter of years), is also an ineffective therapy for this disorder.

Fortunately, sexual medicine has come a long way in the past few years. We now understand this potentially devastating dysfunction much better, and the new brief sex therapy methods have dramatically improved the outlook for men who climax too fast, so that today *over 90 percent of premature ejaculators can be cured within an average of 14 weeks of treatment.* In fact, the results of treatment for PE* are now so good that when I evaluate a troubled single man or couple for a sexual complaint, and the problem turns out to be inadequate ejaculatory control, I feel a little jolt of pleasure in the knowledge that, with rare exceptions, these unhappy people will be enjoying a much more gratifying sex life in just a few months.

In this book I explain what premature ejaculation is and describe the effective new treatment methods. I have also drawn on my experience of treating and curing many hundreds of premature ejaculators over the past 20 years to prepare some guidelines on how couples or single men can use these new sex therapy techniques to overcome this problem by themselves in the privacy of their bedrooms.

---

* The initials PE are often used in medical writings instead of spelling out "premature ejaculation."

2

There are very good scientific reasons to expect that many PE sufferers will be able to improve their ejaculatory control by following these guidelines. But one word of caution is in order. If you conscientiously follow the rules suggested in this book and you do NOT succeed in improving your ejaculatory control, DO NOT DESPAIR. This does NOT mean you are incurable. What it does mean is that in some cases a therapist might be needed to help correct a simple mistake you could have been making in following the directions, or to deal with a deeper emotional problem or some troubles in your relationship which may pose a temporary obstacle to your cure.

So by all means first try your very best to help yourself. You have nothing to lose but your sexual problem. But if this doesn't happen to work for you, please don't give up on yourself. Remember, PE is now among the most treatable medical conditions and the chances are excellent that a reputable sex therapist will still be able to help you.

Go for it.

Good luck.

CHAPTER 2

What Is PE?

The sexually normal male has voluntary control over his ejaculatory reflex. Normal voluntary control does not mean being able to bang away at full speed for hours until his partner comes. No man can do that unless he suffers from the opposite problem, *retarded ejaculation*.* Adequate ejaculatory control refers to a reasonable degree of voluntary control which allows a man to continue to thrust while he is at a high level of pleasure and arousal, until he chooses to "let go" and come. Sometimes he may want an exciting "quickie" and

---

* Retarded ejaculation is a sexual disorder which is the mirror image of premature ejaculation. Retarded ejaculators have difficulty climaxing inside a woman's vagina, with the result that intercourse lasts too long. In severe cases the man does not ejaculate at all.

will enjoy reaching his climax in a minute or two. Other times he may decide to make the pleasure last for five, 10, even 15 minutes. Sometimes men may wish to wait until their partners reach orgasm, and other times they may feel like following their own rhythm, perhaps stimulating their lovers to climax before or after intercourse.

BUT PREMATURE EJACULATORS HAVE NOT LEARNED THIS REASONABLE KIND OF VOLUNTARY CONTROL AND THEY HAVE NO CHOICE. THEY EJACULATE RAPIDLY AND INVOLUNTARILY AS SOON AS THEY REACH A HIGH STATE OF AROUSAL, WHETHER THEY WANT TO OR NOT.

How Fast Is Fast?

In the past, doctors attempted to define premature ejaculation in terms of how quickly the patient ejaculates. Some treatment centers believed that if a man lasted less than one minute after vaginal entry he was premature. Other groups used one and a half minutes or two minutes as their criterion. However, no one can put an exact time period on what constitutes normal or abnormal ejaculatory control. Some men with severe PE may ejaculate as soon as their penis touches the warm, moist vaginal entrance, even before entry, or after just one or two strokes. Others with less severe forms of premature ejaculation come* after 10 thrusts or so, while those with still milder control difficulties are able to hold out for as long as one or two minutes. Finally there are some men who suffer from inadequate ejaculatory control even though they may manage to last for four minutes or so, or even longer. Instead of the natural, easy control which men with normal functioning enjoy, men with this type of PE have to struggle to hold back, and can only do so with tremendous effort and with a great deal of tension, which takes all the pleasure out of the act for themselves and also spoils it for their partners.

Masters and Johnson, who were the first sex therapists to emphasize the importance of the couple's relationship in understanding and treating sexual problems, proposed that a man should be diagnosed as having premature ejaculation if he comes before his sexual partner does more than 50 percent of the time.

The trouble with this definition is that 75 percent of perfectly normal women are not capable of

---

* *Come* is sometimes spelled *cum,* and refers to the *sexual climax,* which is also known as *orgasm,* and in the male as *ejaculation.*

climaxing on vaginal penetration NO MATTER HOW LONG IT LASTS. These sexually healthy women can climax only if they receive direct clitoral stimulation before or after or during intercourse. Since only 25 percent of normal women achieve orgasm with penile thrusting alone, the 50 percent definition does not make any more sense than a specific time period does.

Several years ago, I proposed a new definition of premature ejaculation which has been adopted by the American Psychiatric Association and by the World Health Organization. According to the new diagnostic guidelines, THE ESSENTIAL FEATURE OF PE IS THAT THE MAN LACKS ADEQUATE VOLUNTARY EJACULATORY CONTROL WITH THE RESULT THAT HE CLIMAXES INVOLUNTARILY BEFORE HE WISHES TO.

The key to this new definition is "climaxes involuntarily before he wishes to." The diagnosis of PE should not depend only on how fast a man ejaculates, nor on how his partner responds, but on the QUALITY of his ejaculatory control which should be NATURAL, EASY, and VOLUNTARY.

Under ordinary circumstances, the physical and mental stimulation of making love to his partner causes a man's excitement to rise progressively to the "plateau" stage of sexual arousal (see Figure 1).

they can continue to enjoy rhythmic penile stimulation while staying at the plateau stage, near where orgasm will occur. They can savor their intense sexual pleasure, allowing it to mount slowly or rapidly until they feel

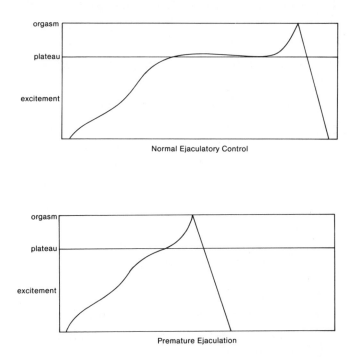

Figure 1. Comparison of the sexual excitement, plateau, and orgasm stages of the sexual response cycle of normal men and men with inadequate ejaculatory control.

rhythmic penile stimulation while staying at the plateau stage, near where orgasm will occur. They can savor their intense sexual pleasure, allowing it to mount slowly or rapidly until they feel like climaxing, without any special strain. By contrast, premature ejaculators become excited very quickly. They are unable to remain at the "plateau" stage of excitement, but come involuntarily as soon as they reach this level.

In other words, a normal man can choose either to stay aroused for a while or to climax rapidly. But the premature ejaculator has no such choice. He peaks quickly and moves right through the "plateau" stage on to orgasm, which puts an end to the sexual experience before he wishes this.

The Destructive Effects of Premature Ejaculation

Ejaculating rapidly is not a problem for all men nor for all partners. Some men don't mind coming quickly once they have entered the vagina and some women are not bothered by their partner's lack of staying power. A number of men simply accept their lack of control. They do not let this spoil their sexual pleasure and, as a matter of fact, many such PErs have active sex lives. Likewise, some women accept their partner's rapid ejaculations, and they take pleasure from other aspects of lovemaking.

Such flexible couples adapt to the premature sexual pattern in several ways, which might be instructive for those of you who are deeply troubled by your problem.

Some women I have seen can follow their partner's rhythm by learning to climax rapidly themselves.

Some men with PE are sensuous, skillful lovers who know how to stimulate their partner to orgasm manually or orally, prior to intercourse or after they ejaculate, or before and after, so that their rapid ejaculations do not interfere with their partner's sexual pleasure.

But far more often than not, PE is a source of distress to the man and to his partner as well. And, unless both partners are very understanding and mature, this condition can have a destructive impact on a couple's sex life and may eventually threaten their entire relationship.

HOW PE AFFECTS MEN

In our society, men often measure their self-worth by the hardness of their erection and by their "staying power." Men who have poor con-

11

trol, especially if they are unsure of themselves in other ways, may end up with a general sense of inadequacy and failure, and may develop additional sexual difficulties.

Secondary Impotence

Not surprisingly, many men with ejaculatory problems lack sexual confidence, and they tend to be anxious about their ability to perform. This is unfortunate because performance anxiety is very disruptive to sexual functioning and often leads to chronic psychological impotence.

PErs who are very distressed by their symptom feel terrible each and every time they come fast. Each negative experience convinces them that they are "losers" and increases their performance anxiety. Then the next time they go to make love, they are even more apprehensive about failing again. But if a man tries to function while he is anxious, he is apt to have problems with impotence because it is *physically* impossible for a man to maintain an erection while he is under stress.

Erection is produced by a high blood pressure system in the penis. When a man becomes sexually aroused, his penile arteries enlarge, increasing the flow of blood into the penis, while at the same time the outflow channels close down. This traps blood within the penis at a pressure high enough to enlarge it and make it hard or *erect*. But if a man should become anxious while he is making love, adrenalin and noradrenalin, the body's "emergency" hormones, are released. These reach the penile circulation in less than one second and instantly reverse the erectile process—the penile blood vessels constrict so that less blood gets in, and the venous outflow channels snap open, which causes the extra blood to drain out of the penis rapidly—leaving it flaccid.

Performance-oriented men with poor ejaculatory control find themselves in a real dilemma. They can decide either to give up their struggle to hold back and simply come fast, which makes them feel awful, or they can make a terrific effort to delay their ejaculation until their partner comes, thereby risking getting so anxious that they flood themselves with adrenalin and lose their erection, which is even worse. I have seen this pattern of performance anxiety lead to a downwardly spiraling cycle of fear of failure and failure and more intense performance anxiety and permanent erectile failure.

Relationship Problems

It goes without saying that PE is not good for your romantic relationships. That is why many of you are now doing something about it.

13

But you should realize that the sexual insecurity, performance anxiety and defensiveness which this problem can cause in men whose self-esteem was not all that solid to begin with can do more damage to your relationships with women than the symptom itself.

The following case is typical.

Al, a 32-year-old accountant, and his new wife, Alice, a pretty, 28-year-old secretary, came to my office because she had lost her desire to have sex with her husband, and was thinking of asking him for a divorce. Al, who loved his wife deeply, was heartbroken and blamed his lifelong problem of PE for their problem.

It turned out that he was indeed a premature ejaculator. The longest he could hold out after vaginal entry was about a minute. Alice had never been particularly troubled by Al's PE. She usually reached her climax on oral stimulation, and although she had reassured Al repeatedly that she was satisfied with this, he became upset and morose each time they made love. All her efforts to comfort him were to no avail, and, not surprisingly, after a while she became less and less interested in making love. When Alice began to avoid sex, Al became very anxious and defensive around her. He constantly put himself down and apologized for everything. This only made things worse between them and soon she began to lose her respect for him.

14

By the time they came to my office, this potentially viable marriage was in a real crisis. Desperate not to lose his wife, Al was convinced that if he could only overcome his premature ejaculations Alice would desire him once more. He did not realize that it was his insecurity and his obsessive, anxious attitude more than his rapid ejaculations which were threatening to destroy the marriage.

Some premature ejaculators don't have any romantic relationships at all. This does not happen because women reject them on account of their PE, but because they develop self-destructive patterns of sexual avoidance. Their fear that they are too inadequate sexually to attract or to satisfy a desirable woman keeps them from leading a normal social life and from finding romance. They often feel so ashamed of their problem that they turn down invitations and dates. Men who fall into the habit of avoiding social and sexual opportunities end up bitter, frustrated and depressed because they are alone and starved for affection while everyone else seems to be in a relationship and enjoying sex.

The saddest case of this sort I have seen was that of a 29-year-old teacher, Bob, who was hospitalized after he tried to commit suicide by injecting himself with insulin. Bob had been a shy, awkward boy. The first time he tried to have sex with a classmate during

15

his senior year at high school, he had come almost immediately. Although his partner, who did not seem to realize what had happened, was not critical, Bob felt extremely upset and humiliated. He never talked with anyone about the incident. He never spoke to the girl again, and he avoided dating any woman for the next 10 years.

He felt inadequate and lonely, and he became more and more despondent as his friends, one by one, were finding girlfriends or getting married.

Three weeks before his suicide attempt, he had summoned all his courage and visited a prostitute in order to try to overcome his problem. He ejaculated even before he fully entered her, and the woman laughed at him. That was the last straw. Bob was mortified and felt hopeless about ever being able to have a normal life and he wanted to die.

What a terrible price to pay when you consider that in all likelihood this young man's PE could have been treated successfully early on, before there was all that damage.

WOMEN AND PE

Women get so much pleasure from foreplay and clitoral stimulation that many do not really mind rapid intercourse all that much. Some women are actually turned on by the idea that they have the power to arouse their lover so intensely that he loses control. But there are women who really crave the feeling of their partner's hard penis deep inside their body and they prefer to have their orgasms during intercourse. And some women, although they are in the minority, are able to climax *only* during intercourse. These are the women who are truly disappointed when intromission is too brief. They often feel frustrated and constricted during intercourse because the partner of a PEr quickly learns that if she begins to get into the rhythm of lovemaking and starts moving her hips freely, her arousal is likely to trigger his orgasm, and end the lovemaking just as she was starting to enjoy it.

Many women who complain bitterly about their husband's PE are really less upset by his rapid climax than by the "wham—bam—thank you, ma'am" syndrome. In other words, women understandably feel bad when a premature ejaculator, because he doesn't know any better or because he is selfish or because he is ashamed of his problem, gives his wife a kiss, feels her body for a little bit, enters her as soon as he has an erection, comes immediately, and turns over and goes to sleep. It is this insensitivity to their feelings, rather than the physical sexual frustration, which is the greatest hurt for these women.

But even if a premature ejaculator is considerate and thoughtful, serious problems are created when a man's sexual dysfunction taps into his partner's hidden insecurities. Women who are sure of their own attractiveness may not be thrilled about their partner's inability to last, but they do not take this personally. However, women who are very sensitive to rejection may feel hurt because they erroneously think that their partner's coming quickly means that he is uncaring or hostile. Even psychiatrists and psychologists used to consider this symptom as a mark of the man's hatred of women. But this simply is not true, as I will explain in Chapter 3 when I discuss the causes of PE. We have found that premature ejaculators are neither more nor less hostile toward women than other men are, and that this dysfunction is really a kind of sexual learning disability.

But even though there is no reality to the myths that their partner is hostile or that only orgasms produced by penile thrusting are fulfilling, I have seen some emotionally vulnerable women who feel terribly hurt, rejected and depressed about their husband's lack of control. Naturally, such deep unhappiness on the part of the partner creates pressures which only worsen the couple's problems.

The next case vignette will illustrate this point.

The couple had been married for two years. Carol, the wife, wept as she told me that her husband, Chester, was a premature ejaculator and that they had not made love for eight months. Chester looked the picture of misery and guilt.

It turned out that Chester usually climaxed about two minutes after intromission. This had been no particular problem for his former girlfriend, who loved oral sex. But it was very different with Carol who would urgently whisper, "Not yet, please—not yet, please—" while they were having intercourse. Then, each time he came, she would sob and hurl invectives at him. Chester was solicitous and caring and tried every way he could think of to give her pleasure. But she refused to allow him to stimulate her genitals in any manner, insisting that only orgasms brought on by intercourse would satisfy her. She would frequently cry that her life was ruined.

Chester had come to feel so guilty about the emotional pain he was causing his wife and felt so helpless about being able to control himself that after a while he could not bring himself to initiate sex at all. Carol, who was extremely insecure emotionally and overly sensitive to rejection, was even more devastated by Chester's sexual avoidance than she had been by his rapid ejaculations.

TRYING TO HOLD BACK CAN SPOIL SEX

The frantic efforts some premature ejaculators make to control their ejaculations can take the fun out of sex. Men who are highly achievement-oriented and competitive are particularly likely to overreact to their sexual "failure" and are apt to try so hard to hold back that lovemaking loses its sensuous quality. Men like Chester, who are desperately trying to satisfy their unhappy partners, also tend to make this mistake.

Premature ejaculators try to hold back in a number of unproductive ways. Some hold their bodies stiffly away from their lover's body during foreplay because they are afraid that if their penis touches her, they might become too aroused prior to intercourse. The result is that the couple's sexual interactions become awkward, stilted and mechanical. Some men concentrate so hard on trying to keep from getting excited that they can't possibly enjoy themselves or give their partners pleasure. In an attempt to avoid rapid arousal, many of these men do not permit their women to touch or kiss their genitalia, which also puts a damper on the experience. Desperate not to come quickly once they enter, they may thrust awkwardly and tensely, which is not much fun for either partner. And if, after all that, he does not succeed in controlling his orgasm (and it is a safe bet that he won't), his anger and his miserable mood will spoil any vestige of joy for both partners. If you have developed the habit of getting morose after you come, you had better try to cut that out. For how can your partner enjoy sex with you if she knows ahead of time that it will always end up with your having a fit?

Worse things can happen to a couple's relationship. If the man becomes too defensive and guilty about his PE, he may begin to avoid sex with his wife altogether, as was illustrated in the case of Carol and Chester. Or worse yet, he may even withdraw emotionally from her. When this happens, any woman will feel rejected and neglected. Especially if she loves him, she may become increasingly frustrated and depressed because of his detachment. By the time these couples seek help, the women are often extremely angry with their husbands. They want to "kill" them or leave them, not so much because they come fast, but because the men have not been open about their problem and because they have avoided seeking help. Unfortunately, these hurts and misunderstandings add up and can undermine a couple's relationship even if they basically love and care for each other.

It is very understandable to want to put off doing something about your PE, and for you to bury your head in the sand with the hope that it will cure itself in time or that you can lick this thing all by yourself. I can also appreciate just how threatening it could be for a man to face what must seem to be a serious sexual inadequacy and what a hassle it is to look for a reputable sex therapist and to make that first difficult phone call.

But you ought to know that it is highly unlikely that your problem will go away all by itself. And you should also bear in mind that the psychological damage your lack of control is causing to your self-esteem, your sexuality, and your romantic relationships will get worse as time passes.

So please, don't wait too long before you do something about your problem. If you are reading this book and are committing yourself to this program, you have already taken that important first step.

CHAPTER 3

What Causes PE?

Premature ejaculation is a disorder of the orgasm phase of the male sexual response cycle. Ejaculation or male orgasm is one of the sexual reflexes. This is quite separate from the erection reflex and from sexual desire which are the other two components of the human sexual response.

Premature ejaculators are by no means sexually inadequate. These men are not impotent. They usually have no trouble attaining firm erections and their sex drive tends, if anything, to be unusually strong and vital. SEXUALLY SPEAKING, PREMATURE EJACULATORS ARE OKAY IN EVERY WAY EXCEPT THAT THEY SIMPLY COME TOO FAST.

The Male Orgasm

The male orgasm consists of two parts—*emission* and *ejaculation.* Emission is caused by a brief contraction of the muscles of the internal male reproductive organs which squeezes semen out of its storage place in the seminal vesicles (see Figure 2), and deposits it into a little reservoir at the base of the penis. The pool of semen is now ready to be ejected and the man feels a certain inner sensation which has been called by Masters and Johnson the sense of "ejaculatory inevitability."

In other words, when emission occurs men perceive a "signal" that tells them that the "gun is loaded" and that the discharge has now been triggered and can no longer be held back.

Emission is normally followed a split second later by *ejaculation proper.* The sensations that accompany ejaculation, which is also called orgasm, range from the most exquisitely pleasurable of human experiences to a simple sense of release. Ejaculation is produced by rhythmic contraction of certain muscles at the base of the penis. These spasms, which occur at a rate somewhat faster than one per second, eject one to five gobs of semen or cum out of the tip of the penis.

Certain biological processes such as digestion, pulse rate, and blood pressure operate *autonomously.*

24

Certain biological processes such as digestion, pulse rate, and blood pressure operate *autonomously*. But ejaculation, like some other bodily functions, such as walking, urination, or talking, is normally under voluntary control. But we are not born ambu-latory or toilet-trained or speaking the King's English or as

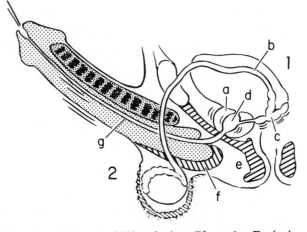

Figure 2. Emission and Ejaculation. Phase 1—Emission: This phase is perceived as the sensation of "ejaculatory inevitability." The internal male reproductive organs [prostate (a), vas deferens (b), seminal vesicles (c)] contract and collect the ejaculate in the urethral bulb (d). Phase 2— Ejaculation: The perineal (e), bulbocavernosus and ischio-cavernosus (f) muscles contract with a .8/second rhythm causing pulsations of the penis and expulsion of the ejaculate. The penile urethra (g) contracts also.

and perfect certain basic functions and reflexes (including our sexual ones) through trial and error and sensory input during the course of our development.

PHYSICAL CAUSES OF PE

Some kinds of sexual disorders, such as impotence and the loss of sexual desire, are frequently caused, at least in part, by a number of medical problems. These include poor penile circulation, hormone imbalances, and the side effects of certain medications. But the cause of premature ejaculation is most often psychological. This is especially true for young men and men who have always had this problem. It is always a good idea to have a doctor examine you if there is something wrong with your sexual functioning and I advise you to do this. But if you have no illnesses and are not taking any drugs and your erections and sex drive are okay, and especially if you have regular medical checkups, you don't have to worry about physical causes.

There is one important exception. Physical problems are likely to be involved if a man who has had adequate ejaculatory control in the past begins to come rapidly. This could mean that he is becoming impotent because of some illness or a drug with sexual side effects, and he is now ejaculating fast before he loses his erection. Also, late-occurring PE can sometimes be the first sign of more serious problems such as diabetes, or a neurological disease—for instance, multiple sclerosis—which damages the nerves that control ejaculation, or a urological disorder, such as urethritis.

Many of the physical conditions which cause sexual symptoms can be treated successfully if the doctor detects them in time. So if you are losing ejaculatory control after you had been functioning well for years, and especially if you are not under unusual stress, please consult a physician who is knowledgeable about sexual medicine, possibly your own doctor or a medical sex therapist or a urologist who specializes in sexual disorders, before you try the suggestions in this book or, for that matter, before you try any psychological treatments.

However, keep in mind that 99 percent of premature ejaculation is purely psychogenic, and most PErs can be cured with the new brief sex therapy methods.*

---

* Recently, a new drug treatment has been developed, by Dr. Mario Gospadinoff of Argentina, which promises relief for those patients with PE who do not respond to sexual therapy. It will be available through physicians in the near future.

THE PSYCHOLOGICAL CAUSES

Until recently, physicians and therapists had many wrong ideas about what causes premature ejaculation. For example, it had long been thought that inadequate ejaculatory control was a kind of impotence and a symptom of a deep sexual neurosis growing out of the patient's childhood problems. Doctors and psychologists were convinced that the little boy's difficulties with his mother and father caused him to harbor a lifelong anger towards and a deep distrust of women, and that these painful early experiences left him with a deep sense of guilt and conflicts about sex and love. It was further believed that the person carries these infantile feelings into his adult life, and that this causes his premature ejaculations. More specifically, therapists operated on the theory that premature ejaculators are unconsciously angry at women and guilty about sex, and that without being aware of this they express these irrational feelings by coming too fast, thereby depriving their partners of pleasure and punishing themselves in the process. Unfortunately, some professionals still cling to this outdated view.

But my experience of working with hundreds of premature ejaculators over the last 20 years has made it clear that there is no reality to this theory. We and other doctors have found that, while some of these men are undoubtedly neurotic and are angry at their partners (which is just as true of men and women who have no sexual disorders), and while such emotional problems can sometimes play into their sexual difficulties, the majority of premature ejaculators have no discernible neuroses or personality disorders, and many genuinely love their wives or girlfriends. Actually, most premature ejaculators I have treated had a compelling wish to become better lovers and were deeply distressed about frustrating and disappointing their partners.

THE IMMEDIATE CAUSE OF PE: INADEQUATE PENILE SENSORY AWARENESS

After studying hundreds of men with deficient ejaculatory control, I have found that apart from any deeper psychological conflicts which might or might not be operative THE IMMEDIATE, "HERE AND NOW" CAUSE OF PE IS ALWAYS A LACK OF SEXUAL SENSORY AWARENESS.

For any number of reasons, premature ejaculators never develop a normal sense of what their genitals feel like when they are highly excited and about to come. It is this *sensory deficit* that is the key to the cause and also to the cure of inadequate ejaculatory control.

A brief look at the science of learning theory should make this clearer. It is an established fact that one needs a certain level of sensory awareness and feedback to learn to control any and all voluntary bodily functions.

For example, it is well known that a child needs the feedback of hearing the sounds he or she makes in order to learn to speak. Deaf children find it difficult to learn to talk because they cannot hear the words. As another example of how acquiring control over bodily functions requires sensory input, is the fact that it is possible to cure bedwetters simply by raising their awareness of what it feels like to have a full bladder. And you know that without the feedback of seeing where the ball lands, you could never master the art of golf, tennis, or bowling.

The same learning principles of sensory input and integration also apply for mastering the ejaculatory reflex. The first few times boys masturbate or have sex with a girl they often get so excited that they climax before they fully realize what is happening. That is perfectly normal. But in the usual course of events, they gradually become familiar with the sensations of their rising sexual excitement which enables them to learn how to make the pleasure last. However, this learning process goes awry in premature ejaculators. For a number of different reasons, these men fail to develop the sexual sensory awareness it takes to acquire ejaculatory control:

- Some men simply get too intensely excited to register their penile sensations.

- According to Dr. William Masters, the first sexual experiences of some of his PE patients took place in tense situations such as the back of a parked car or on the couch of their girl's living room while her parents were upstairs. These boys had an ear out for possible interruptions and they "tuned out" everything else, including their sexual feelings. They finished as quickly as possible and never got out of the habit.

- Other PErs remain unaware of their sensuous feelings because they are too concerned about their sexual performance. These men are in an inner contest to get the highest "grade" as lovers, instead of relaxing and fully enjoying their sexuality.

- Many PErs feel too pressured about pleasing

their partner. During the sex act, their minds are so filled with fears of being criticized or rejected and with checking out their partner's responses that there is no way they can possibly stay in touch with their own sexual sensations.

- Some men feel too guilty about masturbation, about having sexual intercourse, or about their sexual fantasies to allow themselves to register their feelings of pleasure.

These overly excited, anxious, or guilty men concentrate on their negative feelings and tune out their erotic sensations. They avoid prolonged periods of arousal, and they never really become familiar with or comfortable with or let themselves really enjoy the natural feelings of intense erotic pleasure which occur just before the sexual climax.

In summary, you probably came fast since the first time you had sex. But unlike many other young men, who also came fast in the beginning but then went on to develop normal control, you have been repeating the error of avoiding the full awareness of your erotic feelings again and again and again—each time you make love—and you are now stuck with the habit. This pattern seldom corrects itself spontaneously, but the method of systematically heightening the level of sexual sensory awareness which we use in sex therapy is highly successful in accomplishing this.

Are You Always Fast?

You may not be aware of this, but you may not come fast under all circumstances. Chances are that you have poor control only in those situations where you are too anxious or too distracted to tune in to your pleasurable feelings. True, some PErs always come fast—when they masturbate, have oral or manual sex with a partner, or when they have intercourse, but they are in the minority.

More often than not, PErs have better control during masturbation or during oral sex, but they get so rattled about intercourse that they come too fast in that situation only.

If your lack of control is confined to vaginal penetration only, think for a minute about what this implies. Ask yourself what it means if your penis is able to hold out without any trouble while you are stimulating it yourself, but you cannot control that *same organ* when it is receiving similar stimulation in your partner's vagina? Doesn't that prove that you are capable of better control? The situational nature

33

of your problem is clearly due to a simple difference in your mental attitude. When you are by yourself you are calm and just having fun; when you are trying to "perform" for your partner, you become too tense to stay with your pleasurable feelings. And that is what we are going to try to change.

Deeper Causes of PE

APART FROM THEIR POOR EJACULATORY CONTROL THERE IS NOTHING ELSE PSYCHOLOGICALLY WRONG WITH THE MAJORITY OF PREMATURE EJACULATORS.

But, of course, some men with control difficulties also suffer from underlying sexual conflicts which have their roots in certain childhood experiences, and some are having too many difficulties with their partners to be able to function normally.

DEEPER CAUSES I:
ANTISEXUAL CHILDHOOD MESSAGES

Among the most common deeper emotional problems we see in people with sexual disorders is guilt or shame about sexual pleasure. These are left-overs from old "messages" that sex is disgusting, sinful, and harmful which are transmitted to chil-

34

dren by some puritanical families, schools, and churches. Such early antisexual "programming" tends to remain with a person into his adult life and will put a damper on his sexuality even if he no longer believes this old propaganda intellectually, and even if he is not fully aware that he harbors these feelings.

DEEPER CAUSES II:
A TROUBLED FAMILY ENVIRONMENT

Some people still carry emotional scars from growing up in neurotic families, and that is another source from the past which can lead to sexual difficulties. Rather than buffering their children from the stresses of the world as they should, some immature parents use their children as pawns in their fights with each other. Others, who themselves have emotional problems, lay their anxieties and depression on their kids. Some mothers and fathers even act out their own craziness by behaving in an inappropriately sexually seductive or competitive manner with their child. Kids from such troubled families grow up with distorted ideas of sex, love, and marriage, and may have difficulties establishing normal romantic and sexual relationships when they grow up.

Still other parents, with sexual hang-ups of their own, stunt their children's sexual development by punishing them harshly for masturbating, or by threatening them with dire warnings at any display of their normal sexual feelings or curiosity. This gives kids the idea that they are bad if they enjoy sex and sets them up to feel guilty and anxious anytime they get aroused for the rest of their lives.

If you grew up in an unhealthy family environment, there is no point in getting angry at your mother or father. Parents do the best they can, but their own limitations may have resulted in their emotionally abusing you when you were an impressionable kid, to the detriment of your later sex life. There is also nothing to be gained by feeling sorry for yourself. Just get on with your life. Fortunately, the damage can most often be repaired, but only if you take responsibility for doing so for yourself.

DEEPER CAUSES III:
IS IT YOUR PARTNER'S FAULT?

Most often, poor ejaculatory control is not confined to one particular partner. In other words, most premature ejaculators have ejaculated rapidly with all the women they have made love to since they have become sexually active. And most of these men have the identical pattern of rapid uncontrollable ejaculations no matter how they feel about the particular person they are in bed with.

However, there are some men who lose control only with certain kinds of partners. Some men come fast only when they are with a demanding woman. Such men have better control when their lover is very reassuring, while this is no help to others. Some men completely lose control when they are intimate with a woman. These men do better with strangers or with partners they look down upon. Some men with PE, just a very few who have sadistic tendencies, have good control and enjoy sex more when they are hurting or dominating their partner.

But far more often the opposite is true and it is a matter of great frustration to these men that they have the least control when they care the most, and when it is really important to them to please their partner. For the harder a PEr tries to control himself, the quicker he will usually come. And naturally a man will try extra hard to hold out until his lover reaches her climax if he loves her and the relationship is very important to him. What these men often do not realize is that most women cannot climax with penile penetration alone, even if the man can stay hard indefinitely, because they require or desire direct clitoral stimulation. So the pressure to last is often self-imposed and not based on the reality of his partner's needs. This will be explained more fully in Chapter 4.

Some women are calm and supportive, while others become upset when a man comes rapidly, and this can influence the man's sexual behavior. Men whose first sexual partner or partners made a fuss about their PE tend to avoid sex, at least for a while, while those with supportive partners may keep on having sex even though they come fast. But while a flexible partner can make you feel better, this will NOT cure your premature ejaculations. So please do NOT blame your partner for your problems.

However, while the partner *does not cause PE*, her attitude can make a significant difference in how difficult it is to cure this symptom and how much emotional pain it causes.

Women who take their lover's rapid ejaculations as a personal rejection or affront, or women who insist that they can be satisfied only with lengthy intercourse, or those who make it clear that they expect their man to hold out until they have their orgasm even though they know full well that he can't help coming fast create a tense pressuring atmosphere for the premature ejaculator which, to say the least, doesn't help.

The following cases will illustrate some typical partner reactions and how this affects the problem. The first case shows how a supportive partner helps.

Dorothy was a sensitive woman who tried to reassure David, her boyfriend, that he should stop worrying so much about coming fast. "Doctor, I keep telling him that I love him, and that I don't care if he comes fast. He doesn't seem to believe me when I tell him that I'm really very attracted to him."

But David was a nervous worrier and he kept punishing himself and obsessing about his PE. Dorothy's reassurance did not cure him, but her total acceptance of him plus her willingness to join him in sex therapy to work on his problem was very helpful. With the cooperation of his loving partner, David was cured of his PE in 14 sessions. Not surprisingly, he then found other things to worry about.

The next case illustrates how partner pressure can aggravate a premature ejaculator's problem.

Ellen, age 38, was a beautiful woman who had always been nervous and sensitive. She had had many relationships with men. Although she had enjoyed sex with several of her lovers, somehow things never worked out for her. Finally she met Ed, a 46-year-old widower who was crazy about her, wanted to take care of her, and asked her to marry him. But Ed had always been a premature ejaculator and this upset Ellen very much.

Ellen's obsession with Ed's rapid ejaculations began to spoil the good times they had been having together outside of the bedroom. He tried his best to delay his ejaculations—he bit the insides of his cheeks while they were having intercourse, and he tried to think about non-erotic topics like business and sports. But this did not work, and he was now coming faster than ever.

Ellen insisted that Ed get help, and he was more than willing. But Ellen took her partner's sexual symptom as a personal rejection and she became too emotional to be able to cooperate properly in sexual therapy. She could not bring herself to stimulate Ed with any tenderness or feeling. Despite this, Ed's control began to improve. At that point she refused to continue with sex therapy. "It's his problem, Doctor," she told me, "I simply can't put myself through this kind of stress anymore."

Ed consulted me again two years later. He had broken up with Ellen, and was now seeing Edith, who was a sexually secure woman with a calm, stable personality. However, Ed's ejaculatory control was still unsatisfactory. But this time, with his cooperative new partner, his control rapidly improved with sexual therapy.

The Inability To Communicate

In our uptight society people often find it difficult to talk openly about sex. For example, I continue to be astounded when I take a couple's sexual history to find that although they have shared their lives for a quarter of a century or more, have raised children together, have overcome crises, and have been open with one another in all other respects, they have never really discussed sex and they don't even know what each other's sexual fantasies are.

It adds to the problems created by PE when a couple can't talk to each other comfortably about sex. Because while the ability to communicate will not cure PE by itself, straightforward, calm, nondefensive communication is the greatest tool for limiting the damage that can be done by premature ejaculation as well as by other sexual difficulties. But if a couple lacks good communication skills, these problems can escalate to the point of destroying their sex life and their relationship.

Insight Does Not Cure PE

Unfortunately, understanding the deeper emotional problems and the sexual guilts which you picked up during your childhood will not cure your premature ejaculations, even if these originally caused your problem. Neither will facing up to your marital troubles. While such insights are extremely helpful in other respects, you will have to deal with your symptom directly in order to gain control. The following chapters describe how you can do this.

CHAPTER 4

The New Treatment

THE ACTIVE THERAPEUTIC INGREDIENT OF THE
MODERN TREATMENT OF PE AND THE KEY TO ITS
SUCCESS IS THE ACQUISITION OF FULL SEXUAL SEN-
SORY AWARENESS.

To put it another way, unless the doctor can
help the patient learn to focus on the pleasurable
feelings that emanate from his genital organs during
the intense state of sexual excitement which precedes orgasm, therapy will fail, no matter how clearly
the patient comes to understand that his disturbed
family damaged his sexual development, no matter
how much insight he gains into the guilt-provoking
antisexual programming of his childhood which
messed him up, no matter how much his marriage improves, and no matter how well he and his
partner communicate.

Psychoanalysis and marital therapy deal only with deeper conflicts but neglect this key issue of raising the patient's sexual awareness. That is why these methods are not the right treatment for PE, although, being a psychoanalyst myself, I know that they are excellent for many other kinds of psychological and marital problems.

These long-term therapies make the mistake of working only on the patient's unconscious sexual and emotional conflicts or on the couple's hidden neurotic interactions. They trace these problems back to their early origins, on the theory that once the patient understands how his deeper fears and self-destructive tendencies developed as a result of his childhood experiences, he will automatically attain normal control.

But this happens only occasionally. More often than not, although patients' careers and relationships frequently improve in response to the long-term insight psychotherapies, at the end of treatment they mostly still come too fast.

That is not to say, of course, that unconscious neurotic conflicts are never important issues in the treatment of PE. In some cases, but by no means the majority, emotional problems and old scars from childhood, which the patient may not even consciously recognize, cause him to become so threatened or anxious or vulnerable or guilty that he is simply not able to cooperate with, nor benefit from, a sex therapy program unless his deeper problems are also attended to. If this is the case, or if the couple's deep-seated marital problems create obstacles to the dysfunctional partner's sexual improvement, the therapist helps them with these issues during the office sessions.

The Sex Therapy Approach to PE

The new sex therapy uses a combination of sexual exercises which the couple or the patient alone carries out in the privacy of the bedroom and office sessions with the therapist which serve a variety of "backup" functions.

Different exercises are used to treat different sexual problems. For example, women who are not able to have orgasms are given a series of assignments which teach them proper physical stimulation, how to stimulate themselves properly, and how to turn on psychologically. On the other hand, the program prescribed for impotent men deemphasizes sexual performance, substituting instead the goal of mutual pleasuring. This helps them get over their performance anxiety, which is the most common immediate cause of psychological impotence.

Still another set of exercises are used for the treatment of PE. These are designed to correct the man's deficient sexual sensory awareness which, as I have stressed, is the immediate cause of this sexual problem. The sexual exercises should be done on a regular basis and the couple is usually asked to set aside two or three one-hour periods each week for this purpose.

The office sessions, which the couple usually attend together on a weekly basis, are devoted to clarifying the assignments and, if needed, to brief active psychodynamic therapy methods to "by-pass" or resolve the couple's deeper emotional and marital problems which can sometimes get in the way of treatment. But, in contrast to the long-term psychotherapies, when we treat PE we often find it quite unnecessary to delve deeply into the patient's past in order to cure his symptom. And when we do have to do this, in case a patient is not making sufficient progress, we explore these early issues only to a limited extent, just enough to get therapy going again.

RAISING SEXUAL CONSCIOUSNESS

Premature ejaculators have often tried very hard to control their ejaculatory responses, but they, as well as some professionals in the field, go about it the wrong way. These men try to think about baseball or concentrate on their tax returns while they are thrusting inside their lover's vagina. They make an effort to slow themselves down by biting the insides of their cheeks. They drink. They use two condoms, or, sometimes at a doctor's suggestion, they purchase anesthetic ointment to dull their penile sensitivity. Others compensate for their rapid ejaculations by coming twice. True, the second time is usually slower. But as was explained in Chapter 2, this works only when a man is young. After a certain age, men simply cannot come twice in quick succession; if they push themselves, they often end up with performance-anxiety impotence.

All these methods are on the wrong track because they slow the man down by REDUCING his sexual desire, pleasure, and excitement, when what he really needs to accomplish is to PROLONG his pleasure by learning to stay in control while he is highly aroused and excited. As a matter of fact, methods which distract the man from his penile sensations ultimately make the problem worse because they interfere with his sexual sensory awareness even further.

THE PENILE SQUEEZE AND
STOP-START METHODS

Two effective behavioral techniques have been developed which systematically raise the premature ejaculator's level of penile sensory awareness, which, once again, is the necessary ingredient for curing this disorder. These are called the *penile squeeze method* and *stop-start stimulation.*

The squeeze method, which was developed by Masters and Johnson, teaches the man to focus on his penile sensations by having his partner squeeze his penis with her hand hard enough to make him partially lose his erection when he is close to ejaculating. The stop-start method achieves the same goal by systematically having the man interrupt his partner's stimulation of his penis just before he reaches orgasm.

Both methods are extremely effective, but I personally favor the stop-start technique of interrupted penile stimulation. There are two reasons for my preference. First, some men are understandably reluctant to have their penis squeezed, fearing that this will hurt them, and many women are also uncomfortable about doing this. Also, intermittent manual stimulation feels more natural than squeezing the penis, and finally, it is easier to move from manual to intravaginal control from the stop-start method.

The stop-start technique, which was first described in 1955 by the urologist Dr. James Semans, was a real breakthrough in the treatment of premature ejaculation, but for many years it was pretty much ignored. Since that time we have learned a great deal more about human sexual response and sexual disorders. This new understanding has made it possible for us to further improve and refine this method and it is now used widely by sex therapists.

Here is how this is done in clinical practice.

The couple is given the following directions:

Step 1—Stop-Start Manual Stimulation

"When you go home tonight, give yourself some time just for yourselves. Arrange matters to make sure that you won't be interrupted. Don't answer the telephone, turn off the T.V., and don't let the kids into the bedroom. Then take your showers and go to bed without clothes on and with the lights turned low.

"Start kissing and caressing each other's bodies as you normally would to become aroused. As soon as you [*to the man*] have an erection, turn over on your back and close your eyes.

"I want you [*to the woman*] to stimulate his penis rhythmically—up and down. You [*to the man*] guide her hand to show her how fast, how firm, and how deep you like the strokes.

"While she is stimulating your penis you must ignore her for the moment. Don't worry if she is enjoying this or if her hand is getting tired. You must focus only on the sensations of your penis and pay strict attention to your rising excitement. This may seem selfish to you. But absolute concentration on your erotic sensations is critical for this learning process. Besides, this is only temporary. You will give her her turn later.

"When you feel that you are near orgasm but before you get to the point of ejaculatory inevitability, ask her to STOP. Then, when your arousal comes down to a controllable level, let her know that she should start once again. But don't wait too long to ask her to start stimulating you again. Interrupt the penile stimulation just for a few seconds, maybe five to

Figure 3. The Manual-Penile Stop-Start Stimulation Exercise.

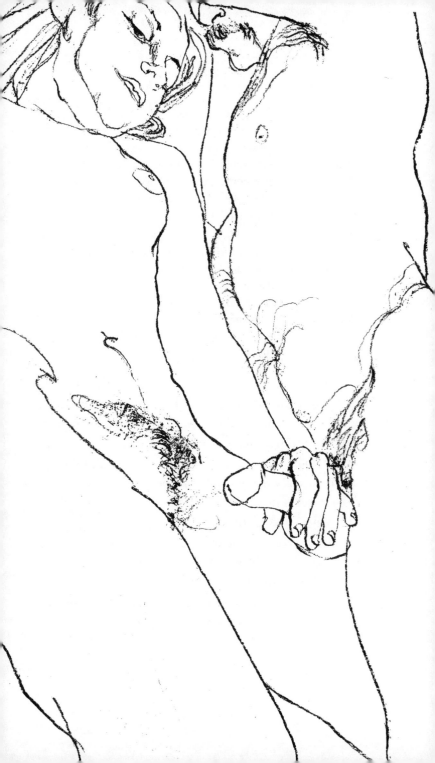

twenty—NOT long enough for your erection to go down but just long enough for the excitement to wane a little. When your sense of excitement has come down to manageable levels, ask her to START stimulating your penis again, interrupt again for a few seconds when you feel that you are close to ejaculating and then ask her to resume. Stop and start three times and allow yourself to come on the fourth time. Remember—DON'T TRY TO HOLD BACK—just focus on the pleasure. Control will come automatically after a little while.

"If you continued stimulation too long and ejaculated before you wanted to, don't worry, that is not a failure. That is merely a learning experience. Next time you will be able to judge better."

Don't neglect your partner. Some women are in a better frame of mind if they have an orgasm before they carry out the exercises. Others prefer to have some sexual attention after their partner has come. Ask her if she would now like you to stimulate her to orgasm—orally or manually, or perhaps with a vibrator. Let her know (if this is true) that you would really enjoy doing this.

Some women just want to be held and caressed after they have brought their partner to orgasm. They feel uncomfortable having their partner stimulate them while he is no longer aroused. Others find the penile stimulation exercises exciting and want you to bring them to climax. Be tender. Give her her choice. You probably don't fully realize how important your approval, appreciation, and consideration are to her.

The couple is asked to repeat the exercise two or three times a week, until they are comfortable with this procedure and confident that they have mastered control on manual stimulation.

Manual stop-start is then repeated a few times more using *vaseline* as a lubricant. Lubricated stimulation is much more sensuous and feels much closer to the sensations of being inside the slippery, moist vagina than the dry hand does. And, of course, the aim of treatment is to transfer control from the hand to the vagina.

Step 2—Stop-Start in the Female Superior Position

When the couple has mastered control on lubricated manual stimulation, they are ready to proceed to the next step: stop-start in the female-superior position (see Figure 4).

Most men find that their arousal peaks most rapidly and their control is worst when they are on top of their partner and are thrusting down. For this reason we usually begin the process of learning intravaginal penile awareness in the female-superior position, which is the easiest one for most premature ejaculators.

The couple is instructed to begin lovemaking as they usually do—by kissing, caressing and, if both are comfortable with this, by using manual and/or oral* stimulation until the man has a good, hard erection, but before he gets overly aroused. Then he turns on his back with his eyes closed to shut out all distractions, just as he had for the manual stop-start stimulation. His partner then sits astride on top of him on his thighs, and then she gently inserts his penis into her vagina by lowering herself onto his erect penis—and "sitting" on him.

She sits quietly for a while with his penis inside of her without moving. This allows the man to focus on how good his penis feels inside the vagina. He then places his hands lightly on her hips and when

---

* You should never do anything sexually which is physically painful or morally or emotionally repugnant to you. If you don't like oral sex, there are plenty of other pleasurable things you and your partner can do.

Figure 4. The Female-Superior Stop-Start Exercise.

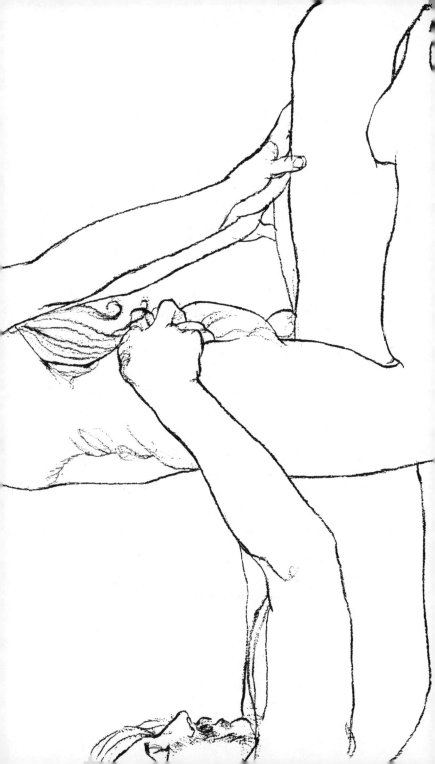

he feels in control he gently guides her movement up and down, up and down, until he senses that he is close to coming, but before he has passed the point of "no return." He then motions her to stop and she sits quietly on him once again for a few seconds with his penis inside her vagina until his arousal abates, then he signals her to resume the up-and-down motion once more. She interrupts her movements twice and he comes on the third time.*

It can take anywhere from two to 10 and even more repetitions of the female-superior stop-start exercises for the man to become familiar with this experience and to learn to recognize the sensations he feels just prior to orgasm while he is inside the vagina. By this time the man's control has usually increased to where the periods of stimulation have lengthened to five or more minutes.

Up to now the man has been lying still on his back while his lover is doing the moving. Now he is told to move his pelvis and to thrust into his partner's vagina actively while she sits quietly on top of him. Once again, he is told to thrust until he feels the

---

* We advise three pauses during the manual stimulation phase of training. During the female-superior exercise this is reduced to two interruptions so that the woman does not tire.

by now familiar pre-orgasm sensations, then he stops for a while, resumes thrusting, and lets go and comes on the third time.

Step 3—Stop-Start in the Side-to-Side and Male Superior Positions

After he is able to stay at the plateau stage for several minutes without coming involuntarily, or without having to stop after every few thrusts, the couple may then be asked to repeat the intravaginal stop-start exercises in the side-to-side position (see Figure 5). This is more rapidly arousing than the female-superior, but not as difficult as the male-superior position.

In some cases, when progress is very rapid, we proceed directly to stop-start intercourse in the male-superior position. Again, most men find that lying on top of their lover and thrusting deep into her body is the most exciting position of all, but it is also the position in which they have the greatest difficulty in delaying orgasm. However, by staying with the discipline of focusing on their erotic sensations and stopping and starting, the great majority of PErs eventually gain control, even when they are on top.

Step 4—Slowing Down

When the couple have learned to feel good about intravaginal stop-start *in their own preferred intercourse position* and control has improved considerably, they are now asked to go to the final step which entails SLOWING DOWN the thrusting instead of stopping entirely. During the slow-fast phase of treatment, the man thrusts at his favorite pace, while focusing on his sensations until he feels that he is near orgasm. Then, instead of stopping altogether as he had been accustomed to doing, he is told to thrust very slowly until his excitement comes down from its peak to a more manageable level. Many of my patients feel wonderful at this point as they learn that they can control their orgasm simply by varying the speed and vigor of their thrusting.

Using these techniques at home, along with psychotherapeutic support and exploration of resistances during the office visits, over 95 percent of premature ejaculators attain satisfactory ejaculatory control (which means the ability to make the plateau stage last without having to stop or even to slow down to the point of interrupting the rhythm of

Figure 5. The Side-to-Side Position Exercise.

lovemaking) within an average of 14 sessions of sex therapy. These are excellent results when you compare this to the 25 percent cure rate which reportedly occurs after many years of long-term psychotherapy.

INVOLVING THE PARTNER

I have said this before, but it bears repeating: A sexual partner is never the *cause* of a man's inadequate ejaculatory control. That is a problem which lies within the man himself and it usually surfaces with every woman he makes love to. But the partner's constructive attitude is crucial for the success of treatment. Our extensive clinical experience has taught us that it is virtually impossible to cure a premature ejaculator if his wife or girlfriend is uncooperative.

For this reason, and also because the wife's feelings and needs should be just as important to a therapist as the husband's, we make a real effort to understand and be sensitive to the wife's emotional needs, and we make sure to enlist her as an active and willing partner in the process of treatment.

In the next chapter I will give you some guidelines on how you can do this without the help of a therapist.

CHAPTER 5

How To Be Your Own Sex Therapist

The principles described in the foregoing chapters can help you improve your ejaculatory control on your own, without a therapist. This chapter tells you how.

We have seen that the special "homework" assigned to patients with PE is designed for the specific purpose of heightening their awareness of their pleasurable sexual sensations premonitory to orgasm in a gradual and systematic manner. The premature ejaculator and his partner practice two or three times a week by themselves at home and, at the same time, they see the sex therapist, usually once a week, so he or she can support their efforts and explain the assignments and correct any mistakes they may be

61

making. The therapeutic sessions also provide the perfect opportunity for dealing with any hurt feelings, misunderstandings, and frustrations which can sometimes arise as a couple engage in the highly charged sensuous and erotic experiences that are entailed in sex therapy.

If you want to be your own sex therapist, you will not have the benefit of the therapeutic backup that a doctor can provide. Fortunately, this is frequently not really necessary. Many couples experience little difficulty in doing the exercises, which after all are the CRITICAL ELEMENT in the treatment of PE. Therefore, there is every reason to believe that, with some guidelines which are described in the following pages, many of you will be able to follow the exercise program successfully and overcome any little snags which may come up by yourselves.

Starting by Yourself

Sex therapy was originally designed by Masters and Johnson only for treating couples. Single men were usually told that they could not be treated for their sexual problem until they found a partner to work with or they were assigned a "surrogate" sexual partner. But now the danger posed by the sexual transmission of AIDS has made it unconscionable for doctors to advise their patients to engage in sex with partners whose HIV* status they do not know. For this reason, we have adapted the same basic penile stimulation exercises which were meant to be used by couples for single men. Since they have no partner to work with, we start the sexual consciousness raising of single men with PE without partners with self-provided penile stimulation. We have found this approach so beneficial that we are now increasingly asking even married men to start practicing the exercises by themselves before we bring in the spouse. Fortunately, it just so happens that the solo exercises are ideally suited for beginning YOUR program of "sexual self help" whether you are single or coupled.

If you are single, you *could* wait until you find the right partner and then do the exercises with her. But you are probably much better off to start improving your control on your own. The sexual confidence you are likely to gain from this will make it easier for you to look for the right woman. And you will be in

---

* HIV stands for the Human Immunodeficiency Virus which causes AIDS. People who test positive for HIV may not have AIDS, but they can infect others through sexual intercourse.

a better position to complete the process of gaining intravaginal control later on.

But even if you have a willing wife or girl-friend, there are some definite advantages to making some headway by yourself before you ask her to become involved.

First of all, it is absolutely essential for you to be in a calm state when you practice control. The exercises simply won't work if you are too tense. Starting the exercises without your sexual partner has the advantage of sparing you the embarrassment of "doing it wrong" in front of an "audience." It is not unusual in the beginning of the training pro-gram, before he gets the hang of the exercises, for a man to come before he stops the penile stimulation or for him to pause too long and lose his erection. As a matter of fact, trial and error is an important part of the normal learning process and you need to be free to learn from your "mistakes" without worrying about how your lover might feel. Also, and most important, working by yourself for a little while until you begin to learn how your body reacts frees you to concentrate on your sexual excitement which, after all, is the crucial ingredient for your cure. You can practice more productively with your partner later, after you are confident that you can control your ejaculations on masturbation, without trying to hold back, simply by varying the speed and intensity of your penile stimulation.

But there are certain situations where it is better to begin the program together with your partner right from the start. If your partner is a highly emotional and rejection-sensitive woman, she might feel very much left out when you tell her that you plan to do the exercises by yourself at first. If that is the case, there is no point in upsetting her—it is better to involve her from the beginning than to put stress on your relationship. Or, if you are uncomfortable about masturbating, you might get too uptight to be able to benefit from the solo exercises. In that case also, better go directly to interrupted penile stimulation together with your partner as was described in Chapter 4.

Don't Do the Program in a Haphazard Manner

Before I go on to describe the start-up solo exercises, I must emphasize that if you want these to work you must commit yourself to doing the program in a systematic and disciplined way, just as you would if you were seeing a therapist on a weekly basis. If you just try the exercises a couple of times and then "break training" and skip them for three weeks, after which you try them some more, you are not giving yourself a fair chance to succeed. Unless you are prepared to do the exercises consistently, step by step, two or three times each week, they probably won't do you any good and you might end up more frustrated and discouraged than you were before.

Communication

One more thing. The importance of enlisting the wholehearted cooperation of your partner has already been mentioned in Chapter 4, but this cannot be said too often. You don't have a therapist to help you with asking her to work with you, so you will have to do it yourself. In most cases, if you use your common sense, listen to your heart, and follow these suggestions, you should have no problem.

First and foremost, you should communicate honestly with her. Do not be afraid. A decent woman will not be turned off if you admit your vulnerabilities to her. She will not lose her respect for you if you tell her how badly you have felt about your lack of control and about disappointing her, and how reluctant you were to face your problem. To the contrary, most women feel closer to a man and more loving and protective when he openly shares his inner feelings with her.

Remember, however, communication is a two-way proposition. It is just as important for you to be interested in and understand her feelings and concerns. If you want to enlist her wholehearted cooperation you must draw her out. Make her feel that her wishes are important to you (if they are, and they should be). Hear her out. Put yourself in her shoes and try to appreciate her point of view. That does not mean you have to do everything she wants you to do if she is being unreasonable. It just means that you cannot afford to ignore your partner's feelings because your insensitivity could hurt her and turn her off. Keep your eyes on your goal, while at the same time considering hers.

Also, in the beginning stages of this program while you are practicing manual stimulation, you should, if at all possible, avoid sexual intercourse with your partner. But don't even start your exercises until you discuss this with her, and get her support. If she seems negative about this, it might help if you explain to her the desirability of a brief period of abstinence for the success of this program.

In my experience, most women feel okay about this once they understand, especially if you show her affection in other ways.

But some women are extremely sensitive to rejection and might be threatened by your wish not to make love for several weeks while you masturbate by yourself, no matter how nicely you present this. If that is the case with your partner, don't push it. Later I will describe how you can be flexible and sensitive to her needs, and still accomplish your objective.

Everyone is different and unique; and each person has his or her own special dreams and vulnerabilities. So apart from these basics about male-female communications, I can't give you an exact formula about how to talk with your partner or how to interest her in working with you wholeheartedly. But the guidelines presented in this and the following chapters should help you find the way.

The Do-It-Yourself Sexual Exercises

Again—you should try to abstain from any other sexual outlet during this phase of your self-treatment. Don't masturbate, except for the stop-start practice sessions, and try not to have intercourse with your partner until you have mastered control by manual self-stimulation.

Depending on your age and the strength of your sex drive, you should do the exercises once to three times a week. DO NOT do this more than that, please—compulsive achievement-oriented sex is counterproductive. The idea is to focus on your pleasure, not on your performance score.

Before you begin, review the directions for the manual stop-start exercises with a partner on page 49. The same principles apply for doing this solo, except that you will do the interrupted penile stimulation for yourself.

SOLO STEP 1—FOCUSING ON
YOUR GENITAL SENSATIONS

Get comfortable. Make sure you won't be disturbed. Begin to masturbate in your usual and familiar manner—with your hand, or by rubbing your penis on the bed or between your thighs; lying on your back, side, or stomach; standing up or sitting down; using a light stroke or a firm one; stroking the tip of the penis or the whole shaft.

Now slow down just a little and try to focus on the pleasurable sensations emanating from your penis as you stimulate yourself and as your excitement rises. Try to pay special attention to what it feels like just before you come, just before you reach the emission phase. And then let go and ENJOY your climax.

SOLO STEP 2—STOP-START
PENILE STIMULATION

A day or two or three later, masturbate again under stress-free conditions. It doesn't matter what position you do it in, but this time use your hand only. STOP stimulating yourself when you reach a high level of arousal, near orgasm. Stop for a few seconds—NOT long enough to lose your erection, but long enough for your excitement to go down a little. Then start the rhythmic stroking of the shaft and tip of your penis again. Interrupt three times. Let yourself come on the fourth time as fast and as freely as you can. DURING THIS WHOLE EXPERIENCE, TRY TO CONCENTRATE ON YOUR PLEASURABLE PENILE SENSATIONS. DO NOT TRY TO HOLD BACK.

SOLO STEP 3— "WET" STOP-START
PENILE STIMULATION

Repeat exercise number two every two or three days until you become familiar with the pre-orgastic sensations and begin to feel a bit more control. Men with very severe PE—those who come almost at once—may need 10 or more trials before they are ready to go to the next step. Others seem to learn adequate sensory awareness on self-stimulation after repeating the solo exercise just two or three times. If you need a lot of practice before you master this step, don't worry, the outcome can be excellent even if it takes you a little longer.

Then repeat the sensory-focused interrupted self-stimulation, standing up in the shower. Run warm water and use soapy suds on your hands as a lubricant. This is very soothing and breaks up your old behavior patterns.

Men who feel uncomfortable masturbating in the shower can skip this and stimulate themselves in any position or location, using vaseline as a lubricant instead. This accomplishes the same purpose, namely, learning control on "wet" stimulation which is important because this feels very much like thrusting into the moist vagina.

When you are able to make the pleasure last for about three minutes before you have to stop, you are ready for the next step. But please DO NOT take a stopwatch into the shower with you. Just estimate the time approximately. In order to succeed you must learn to GO WITH THE PLEASURE. Worrying about how long you are lasting interferes with this.

SOLO STEP 4—
SLOW-FAST PENILE STIMULATION

Repeat the stop-start exercise either in the shower, which I prefer because it is clean, slippery, and a new environment for most of you, or, do it with vaseline if you feel more pleasure that way. This time do not stop stimulating yourself when you reach a high level of sexual excitement. Instead, SLOW DOWN the pace of your stroking. At first you may have to almost stop before you regain control. But after a few repetitions you will get the hang of it and learn to control your excitement merely by reducing your speed a little. Later, when you are inside your lover's vagina, and you have gotten a bit too excited, you can just slow down to a gentler rhythm for a little while, just as you are doing for practice now, and you will be okay. This is much less frustrating to your lover than stopping altogether.

SOLO STEP 5—LEARNING TO STAY AROUSED

You are now ready for the final exercise which is best done by yourself before your partner joins you—

LEARNING TO KEEP YOURSELF AT A STEADY LEVEL OF INTENSE SEXUAL AROUSAL.

By this time you should be much more familiar with your sexual sensations. Now, rate the degree of your sexual excitement (not your erection) on a subjective scale which runs from 0–10. Zero is when you are feeling absolutely no excitement at all and 10 is when you reach orgasm. You should have been stopping penile stimulation when you were at about 8½. If you tried to go until 9½, you went a bit too far, and if you stopped at 4 or 5 you ended the stimulation a bit too soon. Remember, the aim of this program is not to keep your excitement down until you want to come. That is no fun at all, and besides that doesn't work. The objective is for you to learn not to ejaculate while staying at the intensely pleasurable sexual plateau stage which precedes orgasm, and to be able to relish the delicious sensations of being highly aroused instead of trying to hold back.

Now go back to the shower (or the vaseline). Stimulate yourself until you reach 6 or so and then slow down until your excitement goes down to 5. Then speed up again to about 7 and try to keep your level of excitement between 5 and 7 for two minutes or so. Again, DO NOT TRY TO HOLD BACK—that interferes with the learning process. You will find that you can control the level of your arousal merely by changing the speed with which you stimulate yourself and the pressure you exert on your penis. After you have stayed pleasurably aroused for about two minutes, increase the speed, let go and enjoy your orgasm.

One word of caution. Do not try to remain at too high a level of arousal at first—8 to 9 is likely to be too close to orgasm.

Practice this until you are able to keep yourself at high levels of excitement without coming for about five minutes. During real life intercourse, most men stay somewhere between 5 and 7, except for brief peaks of 8 or so, until they are ready to go all the way. Few men can or want to remain at 9. By that time most men are eager to come.

ANXIETY

While you are engaging in these sexual learning experiences, you should also make an effort to notice if you are getting TENSE OR ANXIOUS. If you are, DON'T try to do the exercises! It is a big mistake for anyone to attempt to function sexually while in a state of anxiety. Remember, when you are tense, your sexual organs cannot function properly on a physical basis, because adrenalin makes it difficult, if not impossible, for you to make love.

If you find that you are apprehensive—STOP! Collect your thoughts, try to relax, and if you are with your partner talk about your feelings. These methods often reduce sexual stress, but if you can't calm yourself down, do the exercises some other time when you have regained your emotional equilibrium.

This is a very important rule you should always follow, especially when you are with a sexual partner. NEVER TRY TO MAKE LOVE WHILE YOU ARE ANXIOUS OR TENSE. You are only risking failure and frustration.

PARTNER-PROVIDED MANUAL
STOP-START PENILE STIMULATION

You are now ready to ask your partner to join you in doing the exercises. Turn to page 49 and follow the directions described there for Step 1 for couples. (Single men can follow these suggestions when they are ready to work with a partner.)

Open, honest, caring communication is the key to making yourself and your lover comfortable in the bedroom, and to enlisting her complete and loving cooperation. Before you start your exercises, tell her what you are planning to do and be open about your feelings. It might even be wise to let her read this book. Also, it is extremely important that you understand her and that you be sensitive to her feelings. Ask her how she feels, listen to her, and really try to "hear" her. DON'T argue or apologize or get defensive. DO try to see her point of view and also try to get her to see yours.

When you bring up the touchy matter of preferring to start the program with doing the exercises by yourself, explain to her that you are not rejecting her, but that the results are apt to be better if you practice gaining control without an "audience" for a while. Tell her you want to spare her further frustration and also be honest about your needing to be free from the pressure of trying to look good to her and to satisfy her while you are learning control.

Ask her how she would feel if you didn't make love to her or have an orgasm with her for a few weeks while you are practicing your solo exercises. If she protests, or if you sense from the tone of her voice or from the expression on her face that she is hurt or angry about this, be sensitive. Negotiate with her lovingly. Offer to caress and kiss her and fondle her and, if she would like this, you can make sure that she is satisfied by providing her with clitoral stimulation. But ideally, during this phase of the program, you should not ejaculate, except when doing the exercises.

However, some women simply do not have the emotional stamina to tolerate a period of sexual abstinence, no matter how sensitive their partners are and even if the couple have other kinds of physical contact together. If your partner feels like that, you can offer to be a bit flexible and still overcome your problem, although this will probably take somewhat longer. We have found that the method can work even if a couple take turns. One time you can practice by yourself and the next time you can make love together the way you usually do. This is not ideal from a learning point of view, but it is much better than trying to work on your ejaculatory control with an unhappy partner.

If she is entirely too threatened by your having any sexual experiences without her, back down and skip the solo exercises. Start with the partner-provided penile stop-start stimulation assignments which are described on page 49. After all, this approach is commonly used by sex therapists with great success. Involving your partner right away will just give you a little bit more to cope with in the beginning.

But if you are successful in gaining her understanding and support, and are practicing by yourself—don't leave her out. Tell her what's happening. Talk to her when you are making progress and also when you are having difficulties.

Make her part of the process. Encourage her to talk about her feelings and share your experiences with her.

When you have gained enough control for you to do the exercises together with her, remember that your partner has suffered along with you, sometimes for many years. Not only has she been frustrated by your problem, but you probably have not been spontaneous or sensuous in your lovemaking because of your fear of coming too fast. Making love to a bundle of nerves and apologies is not so terrific for a woman.

Also she might be angry at you if you have avoided facing and dealing with the problem. You are only too human if you hope it will go away by itself. But she is also human, and she may well feel that if you really cared you would have bitten the bullet by this time and sought help.

Actually, your lover is going to play the role of

the therapist. She is the one who will do the exercises with you, not the doctor. Even when a couple is seeing a sex therapist, the wife is more important to the man's cure than the doctor is. We therapists essentially just sit on the sidelines "coaching."

And the exercises are not all that much fun for her even if she really loves you and is very willing to help you, and even if she takes genuine pleasure from your improvement. And even if you, as you should, pleasure her after you come. She would probably feel better about the mechanics of helping you learn control if she clearly sees some benefit for herself, perhaps more intimacy and a better sexual relationship with you, at the end of the tunnel.

But although the stop-start exercises can become somewhat mechanical, you can still make the experience pleasurable for your lover if you remember that, if she is like most women, she will like sensuous foreplay, treasure your kisses and caresses, and enjoy coming to orgasm with clitoral stimulation as long as she is secure in the knowledge that you are not neglecting facing and doing something about your rapid ejaculations.

In some cases, we recommend alternating the stop-start exercises with SENSATE FOCUS. Sensate focus is a structured sensuous interaction that was devised by Masters and Johnson for the purpose of shifting the couple's emphasis from performance to the mutual exchange of pleasure.

The couple is told to abstain from intercourse and orgasm. Instead, they take turns caressing each other tenderly while they focus their attention on giving and receiving pleasure. First one, say the husband, turns face down on the bed, while the wife slowly and tenderly caresses his back, starting from the neck and working slowly to the toes. Then he turns over and she gently strokes his face, neck, arms, chest, belly, thighs, legs and feet, but NOT his penis. While she is doing this he lightly guides her hand to indicate to her where and how her touch feels especially good. Then it is her turn to receive his tender, slow, loving body caresses. First on her back. Then on the front, except for her nipples and genitalia.

This simple-sounding assignment is actually a very powerful method for improving a couple's sexual communications and enhancing their pleasure together. The sensate focus experiences are not really necessary for curing PE. For this reason I did not suggest that you and your partner do these exercises as part of the regular training program. But I have included this brief description of the sensate focus exercises here because this can be very helpful and bring you and your partner closer together if you do this once in a while to break up the sameness of doing the stop-start exercises, should this become a problem.

Watch out for one pitfall. Even though your wife or girlfriend has been complaining bitterly about your rapid ejaculations and she truly wants you to improve, your rapid progress can be threatening to her, although she may not consciously recognize this. Should this happen, she may, without realizing that she is doing this, avoid doing the exercises, or act unpleasantly to you, or sabotage the process in some other way. This can occur for a number of reasons. She may be threatened by the idea that if you solve your problem you will no longer need her, or doing the exercises might be making her anxious, or, perhaps, she is angry with you, or she could be in conflict about your lasting longer because of sexual hangups of her own. Even if she goes along with the program, if she has a negative attitude she is likely to do the stop-start exercises in an ineffective manner. For example, one man complained to me that his wife, who was very angry with him, stimulated his penis with obvious disinterest, "as though she was dusting the piano." Not surprisingly, this couple made no progress until they straightened out their difficulties.

Although she may try to cooperate, if she is very angry or upset she will send out such bad "vibes" that, if you are a sensitive man, you will be too distracted to tune in to your pleasurable sensations. *Keep in mind that most of the few treatment failures we have seen could be traced directly to the wife's resistance.* If your partner has reservations about joining you in this program, you too might find it difficult to succeed.

So, if your wife or girlfriend is ambivalent about doing the stop-start exercises with you, don't get angry. That will get you nowhere. Try to understand the basis of her fears. If your relationship is solid, in most cases she will get over it quickly if you are especially reassuring, appreciative, and giving to her.

Be smart, YOU HAVE TO GIVE IN ORDER TO GET. If you want your partner to be caring and enthusiastic about helping you, isn't it time to be more sensitive to *her* feelings?

For Single Men

This section deals with some of the problems faced by single men who are following this do-it-yourself program. However, men with steady partners could also benefit from some of these suggestions.

CHOOSING THE RIGHT PARTNER

You will sense when your awareness and control on self-stimulation have improved to the point where you are ready to go on and work with a partner. If you are not in a steady sexual relationship, you must first find a suitable lover before you can complete your training program. That could be somewhat intimidating to you. Here are some ideas that might help.

The importance of choosing the right woman extends way beyond your improving your ejaculatory control. Everyone needs the kind of partner one can trust and with whom one can be comfortable and open. If the woman you are with does not want to or cannot, for emotional reasons, accept your problem, you really don't want her. Even though she may have some wonderful qualities, such as beauty and brains, she is likely to be critical in other respects as well. Your relationship will never be easy because you will not be able to let your guard down. With a judgmental, demanding or insecure person, you will have to put on an act all the time and you will always have to worry about being rejected or criticized if your performance doesn't meet her standards. You really don't want that kind of stress, do you?

There are plenty of wonderful women who WILL love and accept you just as you are, and who WON'T put you down or make you feel that anything less than a mutual orgasm is second best. And that is the type of partner you should seek, whether you have a sexual problem or not. But you can develop a relationship with a really giving woman only if you feel good enough about yourself to think that you deserve this kind of consideration and happiness. As a general rule, a partner will be only as good to you as you are to yourself.

One more thing. DON'T try to develop a relationship with someone just for the purpose of gaining ejaculatory control. That is not fair. Besides, the anger, hurt, and hassles such exploitative behavior is bound to generate are usually much more trouble than it is worth. Moreover, unless you are a real skunk, you will probably feel so guilty and conflicted about using and hurting someone who is trying to help you that you won't be able to benefit from the program.

You have an alternative. You can be honest and still accomplish your goal. You would be surprised how many women will be willing to go along with you if you honestly explain that you would really appreciate her help if she wishes to give it, but that marriage is not what you have in mind at this time.

DON'T, however, think of yourself as so flawed that you have to accept the first woman who is willing to help you even though you don't find her attractive. That never works out. Not for you and not for her, either. DO wait until you find an attractive partner who finds you attractive also—someone with whom you can have a nice, warm, honest relationship.

And fight your reluctance to meet new people. The right woman is not going to come knocking on your door while you are watching T.V. You have to make yourself go out on dates. Even if you are nervous, ask your friends to introduce you and to invite you to events where there are single women. I have even advised some of my patients who don't know many women to put an ad in a "Personals" column.

When you date, at first take "small steps" which don't intimidate you. Take a new woman out for a drink instead of committing a whole evening the first time you meet her. When you first talk to her, don't try to put on a phoney "Mr. Cool" act. If you are nervous, admit it. Openness is much more appealing to women.

Above all, DO NOT TRY TO TAKE HER TO BED ON

YOUR FIRST DATE. WAIT UNTIL YOU ARE ENTIRELY COMFORTABLE WITH EACH OTHER BEFORE YOU EVEN THINK ABOUT HAVING SEX. Let me assure you, in today's environment of caution about sexually transmitted diseases, no woman will think less of your masculinity if you don't make a pass right away. In fact, they are likely to be very appreciative.

COMMUNICATING WITH A NEW PARTNER

Once you find a potential sexual partner, it is really best if you can be open with her about your PE right from the very beginning. That would make you much more comfortable. But that may not always be easy when you are just starting a new relationship. If you feel that it might not be wise to tell her about your problem right away before you start having sex, and you want to wait until you two are more solid in your relationship, here are some reasonable alternatives. (Actually you may be pleasantly surprised. Your control may be better than you think now that you have been doing your stop-start exercises. But you can't count on that yet.)

If you have decided to postpone telling her about your problem, you can't very well ask her to do the manual stop-start penile stimulation with you. You have to go immediately to the intravaginal stage of learning control.

DON'T lie, but DO be creative about taking the pressure off yourself without alienating your partner.

DO make love to her as sensuously and as tenderly as you can. Remember, women are much more likely to be put off by your detachment and by your anxiety than by your lack of staying power.

DON'T enter her right away. Most women hate to have foreplay end before they have a chance to become fully aroused. Just DON'T rub your penis against her or the bed while you caress her, or you might get excited too quickly.

DON'T penetrate her if you are too aroused. Begin intercourse only while you are moderately excited. If you find yourself too near orgasm, slow down for a while until your arousal comes down to 6 or so before you attempt vaginal intromission.

DON'T thrust rapidly once you enter. Easy does it. Try to create a stop-start or a slow-fast situation without actually telling your partner what you are doing.

After you enter her, you want to stay there quietly for a little while. At the same time, you might let her know how much you enjoy being close to her: "I love the way it feels to be inside you. You are really very exciting to me." After your excitement comes down to around 6, start moving slowly again. You may not realize this, but such "teasing" often heightens a woman's pleasure, and she is very likely to regard you as a superb lover.

If your excitement rises too quickly despite these tactics and you reach a "dangerous" 8½ right away, it is best to pull out and stimulate her body and her erotic zones for a while. You could say something like, "This feels wonderful, but I would love to kiss your genitals (or body, or breasts, or hair, or mouth, or neck) for a while now."* After your excitement has come down a bit, you can enter her again.

DON'T thrust away at full speed while trying to control yourself. You should have learned better by now, and you should know that this is completely counterproductive.

DO try to help her have an orgasm before you enter her—with your hand, your mouth, or a vibrator—as the two of you prefer. This will free you up to focus on your own sexual sensations without guilt. Also, DON'T try to hold out if she gets very aroused while you are inside of her. The quickening of her

---

* Dr. Michael A. Perelman, who is on the faculty of our program, devised this method.

body movements as her excitement peaks is likely to trigger your orgasm. DO try to avoid falling into that trap by satisfying her first before you enter. But if you can't manage that each time, DON'T get tense. If her excitement is too arousing for you, don't fight it. Let yourself come and make sure she has an orgasm afterwards. But for heaven's sake, don't carry on if this should happen. Try to remember that you will soon be able to enjoy your partner's passion without losing control.

DO KEEP YOUR ATTENTION FOCUSED AT ALL TIMES ON YOUR SEXUAL SENSATIONS JUST AS YOU DID WHEN YOU WERE DOING YOUR SOLO EXERCISES. While you are inside her, try to stay between 6 and 7. If you get up to 8½, you either have to think of a creative way to interrupt the stimulation or, if there is no way you can do this at that particular time, you should let go and come with as much pleasure as possible. DO NOT try to hold back. That will only give you a problem.

Again, if you do come fast, DON'T be too apologetic. Play it cool. Your insecurity and anxiety are likely to be a much bigger turn-off for your lover than your coming fast.

DO communicate. If you do come fast, tell your lover that you find her extremely exciting and that you really enjoyed your orgasm (if that is true).

DO be selfish (temporarily). While you are thrusting, focus only on your own sensations. Tune her out.

But DON'T pull away after you ejaculate, even if it was fast and you feel terrible. Women are more offended and rejected by a man's withdrawing from them after he is "finished" than by his coming fast. So DON'T jump out of bed and clean yourself off, and if you are not living together, DON'T look at your watch and rush home. DO caress her, kiss her, offer to bring her to orgasm. Talk to her afterwards. Again, DON'T make her feel used. DO use your head, your heart, your hand, your mouth, or a vibrator.

DO keep on thrusting for a little while after you have ejaculated if your partner likes to come with your penis inside her. Even if your penis is not hard, the pressure of your pubic bone can bring many women to orgasm.* Also, and most men don't realize this, the skin deep inside of the vagina is not sensitive, and most women find it impossible to tell if you are not all that erect or if you have ejaculated.

DON'T try so hard to keep your penis from becoming stimulated during foreplay that you end up making love in a jerky, stiff, or stilted and me-

---

* Method of Dr. Michael A. Perelman.

chanical manner. But again, DO try to keep yourself from rubbing your penis rhythmically against her or against the bed while you are stimulating her, before you enter her. Remember, you DON'T want to be too aroused when you penetrate.

DON'T overestimate the importance of intercourse or of mutual orgasm for your lover's sexual pleasure. It comes as a surprise to many men that most perfectly normal, sexually healthy women climax only in response to clitoral stimulation and cannot come to orgasm on intercourse alone even if this lasts for a very long time.

The myth that normal women climax only during intercourse and that a good lover will insure that intercourse results in simultaneous orgasms has done a great deal of harm to innumerable people's sex lives.

Countless women are too ashamed of their clitoral eroticism to discuss this with anyone. So they go on mistakenly believing that they are abnormal because they don't come on intercourse. Not wanting to disappoint their husbands, many fake coital orgasms, sometimes for years. Since no male can tell if a woman's orgasm is real or not, the husband, thinking he is doing a fine job of pleasuring his wife, never provides her with the stimulation she needs.

These unfortunate women cannot tell their husbands that anything is wrong without admitting that they have been fooling them, and they remain perpetually frustrated. Not surprisingly, many eventually lose their interest in sex altogether.

The mutual orgasm myth is also destructive to men, especially those who come fast, because this adds to their guilt and shame when their wives don't climax on intercourse. Even if they are skillful and considerate lovers who really understand how to caress a woman's body and give her exquisite sensuous pleasure, many premature ejaculators are plagued by pervasive feelings of failure and guilt and by a sense that they are selfish because they are not able to hold out until their partners come.

The truth is, while only 25 percent of women are capable of having so-called "vaginal" orgasms, that is, by penile thrusting alone, the majority, or about 75 percent of PERFECTLY NORMAL WOMEN can reach a climax only if they receive adequate clitoral stimulation. Moreover, many women who do have the ability to climax with penile thrusting alone report that their orgasms are better and more intense with manual or oral "clitoral assistance."

That is why over 99 percent of females masturbate by rubbing their clitoris rhythmically, and NOT by inserting objects into their vaginas.

And that is why, even when you learn perfect control and can last a long time, your partner may still not climax on intercourse.

Of course, there are a few lucky sexual partners who do enjoy coming together. But please keep in mind that the greatest number of sexually satisfied couples, couples who have hot, passionate, glorious sex together, take turns coming.

True, it might be a bit more of a hassle for you to have to stimulate your partner manually or orally, before or after you come, or for her to stimulate herself to orgasm (which is what some perfectly normal couples prefer) instead of her reaching her climax spontaneously during intercourse. But this can also be very exciting and is by no means a "second best" way of making love.

It is NOT true that if she loved you, or if you were a better lover, she would climax along with you. How she climaxes is mostly a matter of her natural response pattern which has nothing to do with her passion for you or with your ejaculatory control.

Finally, before you put yourself down because of your PE, remember that a man's sensitivity to how a woman's body functions, his ability to tune into her erotic fantasies, his skill at foreplay and clitoral stimulation, and his sexual energy are much more important to most women than the size, shape, hardness, and lasting power of his penis.

DO be sensitive to and affectionate and sensuous with your partner outside of the bedroom, as well as in bed.

DON'T be guilty about "using" her to improve your control. Just make sure you DON'T take advantage of her, and that you GIVE HER as much as YOU GET from the relationship.

CHAPTER 6

Avoiding Errors and Resistances

You are overcoming your PE on your own. This will save you the expense and trouble of finding a reputable sex therapist. But this also means that you will not have the benefit of an expert professional to guide you and to correct any errors which you might make or to help you overcome any emotional resistances that might possibly trip you up while you are trying to learn control. But don't be overly worried. Such potential difficulties are not inevitable, nor are they insurmountable, especially if you know what to look out for. Therefore, on the following pages I have listed the most common errors and pitfalls which we have encountered while treating premature ejaculators, along with suggestions about what to do should these surface while you are following the program.

A number of potential problem areas have already been mentioned in other contexts. But in order to present a complete list of precautions all in one place, I have repeated them here and added some others.

Again, you may be able to do the progressive steps of this program without any difficulty whatsoever. However, if you find that your control is not improving steadily, as it should, read this section again, and try to analyze the problem and correct it before you proceed with the next step.

Common Errors You Might Make in Doing the Exercises

1. *Not making a real commitment to the program and doing the exercises in a haphazard manner.* The program will not work for you unless you are prepared to devote yourself to it and follow the directions carefully—step by step.

2. *Making excuses or avoiding the exercises because this makes you more nervous than*

you had realized. It is only natural for you to be anxious. But you must fight your urge to avoid doing the exercises on a regular basis. Avoiding the "homework" assignments is the most common resistance we encounter in treating premature ejaculators and the most common cause of treatment failure. If you make excuses to avoid doing the exercises, and don't stay with it, you cannot possibly overcome your problem.

3. *Skipping steps.* These exercises are effective only if they are done in correct sequence, step by step. Trying to rush ahead will sabotage the learning process. One of my patients tried to have intercourse in the male superior position after only one successful solo stop-start in the shower. Naturally, he came at once, much to his wife's distress and his own discouragement.

4. *Trying to hold back.* Old habits are difficult to change. You are supposed to control your ejaculations only by varying the pace and intensity of your penile stimulation. Holding back is counterproductive.

5. *Concentrating on the length of time you can hold out or on the number of strokes*

before you come instead of focusing on your pleasure. Paying attention to your pleasurable sensations when you are very aroused is the key to the cure of PE. Dwelling on how many strokes or minutes it takes before you ejaculate interferes with your sensate focus.

6. *Continuing the stimulation too long.* You ought to stop stimulating your penis well BEFORE your reach the emission stage of ejaculatory inevitability.

7. *Waiting too long before resuming stimulation during the stop-start exercises.* You should NOT wait until you lose your erection. You should resume stimulation as soon as your FEELINGS of excitement have diminished to a manageable level. Young men can have a perfect erection at 5 or 6, and men 35 years or younger should go down to about 6 before starting the stimulation once more. Older men may begin to lose their erection at about 7 or so. If you are over 50, you have a lower margin for error and you should begin stimulation again at 7½ BEFORE you begin to lose your erection.

8. *Not waiting long enough before resuming stimulation during the stop-start exercises.* Do not resume until your excitement level has come down to 6 to 7½. Starting stimulation again while you are more aroused than that is too close to coming and does not give you sufficient leeway.

9. *Pulling out while stopping during the intravaginal stop-start exercises.* You are supposed to stay quietly INSIDE the vagina while you are pausing.

10. *Thrusting against the bed or against your lover's body while you are stimulating her.* You might get too excited if you do this. You should not commence the intravaginal stop-start exercises if you are over 7. If you should reach a level higher than that, wait till you cool off a bit before entering.

Mistakes in Relating to Your Partner

1. *Trying to do this program with the wrong partner.* No matter how well you communicate and no matter how loving you are, if

your lover does not care enough about you or if she is too anxious or if she is not flexible enough sexually to be cooperative, she could be more of a hindrance to you than a help.

2. *Failing to enlist a potentially fine partner's wholehearted cooperation before you start the exercise program.* Partner resistance is the second most common cause of treatment failure for PE. Trying to do this program with an ambivalent or unwilling partner is a guarantee of failure. If your partner is sexually open and if she cares for you, the chances are that she will help you providing that you take the time and make the effort to explain your situation to her and are considerate of her needs and desires. Also, it is best to get her agreement *before* you involve her in the exercises.

3. *Failure to communicate your feelings or not listening to hers.* Communication is your best tool for enlisting your partner's cooperation and for making both of you comfortable in the sexual situation.

4. *Not being sensitive to your partner's feelings or being out of touch with your own.*

It is difficult to get a woman to commit herself to helping you unless you are sensitive to her feelings, and it also helps to establish an intimate relationship if you are in touch with your own inner anxieties, and conflicts.

5. *Engaging in foreplay in an anxious, mechanical manner.* This will turn her off more quickly than your coming fast.

6. *Withdrawing emotionally or physically after you have climaxed.* This will make her feel rejected and used and is likely to make her lose her enthusiasm about helping you.

7. *Apologizing profusely for your problem after you come or before you make love.* This will probably turn her off completely. Most women like strong men who have a good sense of themselves.

8. *Getting angry or depressed if you come fast.* She will eventually become afraid to go to bed with you if she anticipates this kind of hassle. Remember, normal people like to have FUN in bed. Try to control your sense of frustration and your disappointment.

9. *Being overconcerned with pleasing your partner.* Obsessing about your partner's re-

101

sponse interferes with concentrating on your penile sensations. You cannot overcome your problem unless you "tune out" your partner and "tune into" your own arousal. But only while you are having intercourse—not before you enter nor after you come.

10. *Not volunteering to pleasure her and/or to satisfy her with a clitorally-induced orgasm before or after you climax.* This should and will make her angry with you.

11. *Not appreciating her efforts.* This will set her up to feel exploited and angry with you. She is doing this mainly to please you, and your acknowledgment is important to her.

12. *Not being loving to her outside of the bedroom.* This will destroy a relationship with any woman who feels good about herself.

13. *Having an affair with someone else.* While you are doing this program, stick to one partner. This is also good for your health and your partner's.

14. *Doing things to turn your partner off sexually.* Smoking smelly cigars, drinking a lot, watching TV a lot, going out with the boys a lot, not brushing your teeth, not shaving, not taking a shower, criticizing her, embar-

rassing her, making her feel insecure by flirting with others or by telling her about other women in your life, bringing up anxiety-provoking topics such as her American Express charges, her weight, etc., etc., etc.

How To Tell if Your Partner Is Resisting

If your partner is uncooperative, don't ignore it. Face up to it so you can do something to change her attitude; otherwise, you might not improve. Your partner is probably resisting doing the program with you (although she may not be aware of this) if:

1. *She is avoiding or making excuses about doing the exercises.* She is on the phone all night. She makes numerous dates for the two of you so you are never alone together. She invites the kids into the bedroom. She has to go shopping just when it's time to do the exercises. She plans a trip without you. She takes on extra responsibility at work. She is drinking a lot more, doing drugs, getting fat, etc., etc., etc.

2. *She flirts with other men, goes out without you, has an affair.*

3. *She starts fights or brings up unpleasant topics when you are about to do the exercises.* Taxes, the kids' school problems, your boss, World War III, pollution, your hair thinning out, your table manners, the dentist's bill, etc., etc., etc.

4. *She is angry at you.* She criticizes you excessively, has no time for you, does not make eye contact with you, constantly interrupts you, makes fun of you, complains a lot, and makes unreasonable demands.

5. *She is doing things to turn you off sexually.* She doesn't shower, doesn't shave her legs, doesn't wash her hair, doesn't brush her teeth. She hides behind clouds of cigarette smoke and/or she wears an old bathrobe, wears curlers and/or greasy face cream to bed, etc., etc., etc.

Again, if your partner acts in any of these ways or others which pose an obstacle to a relaxed, constructive, pleasurable sexual ambience, you are not likely to succeed in improving your ejaculatory control.

Don't waste your time feeling sorry for yourself or getting angry at her. Try to find out why she is undermining the program.

- Is she aware that she is doing this?
- Is there something about the exercises that she doesn't like? What?
- Does she have sexual hangups of her own?
- Is she secretly afraid that you will reject her once you function well sexually?
- Is she angry at you for some valid reason? For irrational reasons?
- Is she afraid she will lose control over your relationship when you become sexually more adequate?
- Is she afraid you will give her a hard time once you don't need her for the exercises anymore?
- Does she feel you are using her? Is she right? Or is she imagining this?
- Might she feel, on some level, that she doesn't desire a good sexual relationship?

If your wife or girlfriend seems to be resisting, tell her that you sense that she is unhappy about doing the exercises, and ask her if there is anything you can do to make things more pleasant for her. Loving, open discussions can often allay a woman's fears and deepen her commitment to improving your sexual relationship.

105

How To Tell if YOU Are Resisting

1. *Are you setting your partner up without even knowing it?*

2. *Are you pushing her away emotionally, criticizing her excessively, making her feel insecure, using her, antagonizing her?*

3. *Again, are you making excuses to avoid the exercises?* One of my patients invited his mother to stay with him for two months and then complained that he and his wife lacked privacy for doing the exercises.

4. *Are you "too busy" to do the exercises? Is sex at the bottom of your list? Do you schedule the exercises for the late evening hours when you and your wife are exhausted?* You and your partner must give this program a high priority or it won't work for you. Incidentally, making room in your life for intimacy and love is an excellent idea, even after you have gained control.

5. *Do you let the kids come into the bedroom any time they feel like it?* Many people who are afraid of sex use the children as an excuse to avoid sex and the exercises, with the rationalization that the children would feel

rejected if the bedroom door were closed to them. Children should be secure in the knowledge that their parents are available in real emergencies—if they feel ill or have a nightmare. But they are better off if you set limits, teach them to respect their parents' privacy, and set them an example of how loving couples act.

6. *Are you using TV-watching to avoid intimacy with your wife?* TV is the most common defense against sex in the U.S.

7. *Have you taken on extra work? Scheduled business dinners? Business trips?* Be suspicious. A hidden motive for your sudden enthusiasm for your career could be your anxiety about doing the exercises. It might actually be terrific for you to take a holiday trip alone with your wife or girlfriend. But DO NOT include the kids or invite friends along. Concentrate on improving your relationship and your sex life together while you are free of the usual distractions.

8. *Are you drinking more than usual? Doing drugs? Having accidents lately? Smoking more? Gaining weight? Having bad dreams? Getting into trouble at work?*

107

These could all be signs of sexual anxiety and/or resistance. If any of these things are happening to you, be honest with yourself, face the possibility that something within you is working against your efforts to become sexually adequate. Make yourself stay with the program. Once you get into the routine, these anticipatory anxieties and self-destructive tendencies often go away.

Some Hidden Reasons Why People Sometimes Sabotage Their Own Sexual Success

The following deeper sexual and emotional conflicts, which are the result of old childhood problems of the kinds discussed in Chapter 3, can lead to resistance and sexual self-sabotage. Most people are not aware of these irrational self-destructive tendencies.

1. The exercises are bringing up your old hang-ups about masturbating.

2. The exercises are bringing up your old rebellion against being told to do "homework."

3. The fear of sexual success.

4. The fear of intimacy.

5. Guilt about sexual pleasure.

6. She reminds you of your mother.

7. The feeling that you owe her more than you are willing to pay her for helping you. However, if you were honest in the first place, and your partner willingly chose to help you, you have done nothing wrong. Your old neurotic guilt is tormenting you.

8. The fear that she will, now that she is helping you, want more of a commitment from you or even marriage. If you implied that you might marry her only to get her to help you, you are in trouble and deserve it. But if you were straight with her, these concerns are only in your head and based on your distorted view that women are not to be trusted.

Unconscious sexual sabotage is not uncommon and can often be overcome once you admit what you are doing and realize that you are hurting yourself. Share your feelings with your partner, and make yourself do the exercises despite your urge to skip them. Chances are that your anxiety will go away after just a few practice sessions.

If you and your partner are really committed to improving your sex lives and you are doing the exercises right, you should be making steady progress. If you are not, if you can't get past a certain point, then one or both of you could be resisting in some of the ways I have listed above, or in some others. Sit down and think about it. Better yet, try to figure out, together with your partner, what is gong on. In my experience, if you and your partner face the fact that you are stuck openly and honestly, errors and resistances can be gotten out of the way rapidly and successfully most of the time. However, if the resistances should persist, do not give up, but it's probably time to see a good sex therapist.

A Special Note to the Women

I would like to say a word to the wives and girlfriends. You are doing a wonderful thing for your man by supporting him and by participating in this program. You should be proud of yourself. Don't get hung up on the fear that he will reject you after his ejaculatory control improves. That's probably just your old insecurity coming up again. If you have a good relationship, he will need you just as much as he did before. Don't be threatened. Chances are that if he were going to leave you, he would have already done so. But, if it should turn out that he is a "user," you might as well find out now and get rid of him before you get in any deeper.

In my experience, men really appreciate a woman who accepts and helps them when they are vulnerable. Moreover, working together to improve their sex life in such an intimate way, and letting their defenses down, generally brings a couple closer together and usually deepens their relationship and their commitment to one another. And don't forget, when his control improves, he will become a much better lover and give you a great deal more pleasure!

CHAPTER 7

After You Gain Control

I consider a patient cured when he no longer has to stop and start to control his ejaculations—except perhaps once in a great while, when he is feeling exceptionally passionate or if he is under unusual stress. Once you gain control, you should be able to come when you wish to, and intercourse should be entirely natural and effortless, although like most normal men you might sometimes wish to slow down a bit. You should have gotten over your old habit of trying to hold back and your lovemaking should no longer be spoiled by any apprehension about coming too fast.

You will sense when you have reached the level of control that is satisfactory to you. You will feel confident and sex will feel "right" and easy. And it is not just a matter of HOW LONG you can maintain control. That is important, of course, but THE QUALITY of your orgasms should also improve, and you should feel much more pleasure.

In sex therapy it takes an average of 14 office visits and about 20 to 40 practice sessions at home for a man to gain ejaculatory control. Many of you can also expect to complete the program successfully after 40 or so practice sessions. But don't be discouraged if it takes you a little longer than that because you are working on this alone, without therapeutic backup. Be prepared for as many as 50, or maybe even more, practice sessions before you overcome your problem.

Some of you will have to practice slow-fast intercourse only five or six times before your control becomes good. Others will take a little longer to reach this goal. Some of the patients who have ultimately had the best results had to stay with slow-fast intravaginal intercourse for several months before their control gradually became automatic. So be patient, and stay with it. But, if it takes a long time before you can have natural intercourse without having to stop, don't forget your partner's feelings. After a while, the lack of spontaneity imposed by the exercises can get to be a little tiresome for her. Show her some appreciation for her patience.

There is one thing all of you will have to do for the rest of your sexual lives if you want to stay cured.

YOU WILL ALWAYS HAVE TO FOCUS YOUR ATTENTION ON THE PLEASURABLE GENITAL SENSATIONS WHICH AC-COMPANY YOUR RISING EXCITEMENT. For most of you, this will become so habitual that you won't even realize that you are doing it. A few of you, those who are not entirely comfortable with sexual pleasure, will have to make something of an effort to keep your mind from wandering while you are having sex.

We have found, on the basis of a great deal of clinical experience, that, for the most part, once a man learns good ejaculatory control he will never relapse. If you think about that, it makes perfect sense. Once you learn something, like a language or how to drive, it's yours. And no one can take it away from you.

There are some exceptions. If you should find yourself under unusual tension, which can happen when you are making love with a new partner who intimidates you, or if you are having serious problems in your life outside of the bedroom, you might find yourself beginning to come fast again.

Please don't panic. If this happens more than one or two times, just go back to the stop-start solo exercises for a short while. Better yet, practice a bit with your new lover. Your control will come back very soon.

Readings and References

For those of you who might want more technical information about sexual disorders, premature ejaculation, sex therapy, and related topics, I have listed the following textbooks which are used by doctors and sex therapists.

1. Friedman, M. *Overcoming the Fear of Success.* New York: Warner Books, 1985.

2. Masters, W. H., and Johnson, V. *The Human Sexual Response.* Boston: Little, Brown, 1966.

3. Masters, W. H., and Johnson, V. *Human Sexual Inadequacy.* Boston: Little, Brown, 1970.

4. Kaplan, H. S. *The New Sex Therapy.* New York: Brunner/Mazel, 1974.

5. Kaplan, H. S. *Disorders of Sexual Desire.* New York: Brunner/Mazel, 1979.

6. Kaplan, H. S. *The Evaluation of Sexual Disorders: Medical and Psychological Aspects.* New York: Brunner/Mazel, 1983.

7. Kaplan, H. S. *Sexual Phobias, Sexual Aversions, and Panic Disorder.* New York: Brunner/Mazel, 1987.

8. Kaplan, H. S. *The Illustrated Manual of Sex Therapy, Second Edition.* New York: Brunner/Mazel, 1987.

9. Kaplan, H. S. *The Real Truth about Women and AIDS: How to Eliminate the Risks Without Giving Up Love and Sex.* New York: Simon & Schuster, 1987.